Surfside Style

Surfside Style

relaxed living by the coast

fifi o'neill

photography by mark lohman

CICO BOOKS

LONDON NEW YORK

www.rylandpeters.com

Published in 2020 by CICO Books
An imprint of Ryland Peters & Small Ltd
20–21 Jockey's Fields   341 E 116th St
London WC1R 4BW   New York, NY 10029

www.rylandpeters.com

10 9 8 7 6 5 4 3 2

Text © Fifi O'Neill 2020
Design and photography © CICO Books 2020, except for page 5
© Mark Lohman 2020

A CIP catalog record for this book is available from the
Library of Congress and the British Library.

ISBN: 978-1-78249-880-3

Printed in China

Photographer: Mark Lohman

Editor: Martha Gavin
Art director: Sally Powell
Production manager: Gordana Simakovic
Publishing manager: Penny Craig
Publisher: Cindy Richards

MIX
Paper from
responsible sources
FSC® C106563

contents

introduction 6

quintessential elements 8

colors 10

surfside embellishments 13

furnishings 20

the homes 22

shack chic 24

island vernacular 34

tiny haven 44

seaside zen 54

coastal vibes 64

free spirit 72

serene sensibility 82

seaworthy sanctuary 96

flip flop escape 112

seaside comforts 126

family style 136

classic charm 148

index 158

resources 159

acknowledgments 160

introduction

For many of us the lure of living by the water is the ultimate siren's song. As organic as the ocean and as warm as summer sand, surfside style brings comfort, beauty, durability, charm, and a sense of well-being to interiors and creates a haven from the hectic pace of day-to-day life. Its versatility lends itself to a variety of looks from comfortably modern, to cottage appeal, tastefully rustic, island flair, and a free-spirited attitude that welcome personality, practicality, and poetic beauty.

These dwellings embody feelings of vacations, relaxation, and romantic vibes. Large or humble, they are dreamy sanctuaries that evoke emotion and nurture one's soul. Though their decor varies, these homes share a love of the coast and represent the bright, beautiful, and energizing aura of life on the water.

While prevalent on the beaches of America's Atlantic and Pacific coasts, surfside style can now be seen anywhere and reaches far inland because it is as much a state of mind as a reality.

Surfside style is all about creating calming, airy spaces that beckon with an easy-going, restorative, and seductive laid-back mood. But it is also about the connection with nature through outdoor living areas, beautiful views, and organic materials. With their soothing colors and cozy informality, *Surfside Style* homes, and sand and sun-lovers, live in blissful harmony with their surroundings.

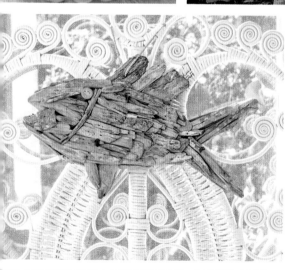

quintessential elements

colors

For an environment that feels equally soothing and inviting, nothing beats classic hues ranging from deep and soft blues to neutrals like sandy tones, whites, buttercreams, and soft grays. For a lively and fun mood, cheerful and vibrant colors that take their cue from sunsets and citrus hues do the trick. Whichever combination appeals to you, one thing remains constant: when you live by the water you can't help but be inspired by your surroundings.

SUNSET HUES

LEFT: Just as artists are inspired by nature, you can look to the outdoors for inspiration and for unexpected color combinations to re-create indoors. This room's accents bring to mind the fiery reds, oranges, and blues of an island's summer evening skies.

These brilliant hues can be overwhelming on a large scale so dabble in sunset tones via a piece of furniture or smaller accessories. Peach pillows, bright green and orange chairs, and vivid red pendant lights add a tropical punch and create a sunset-like layer, while the crisp white walls and ceiling soften the effect and keep the room feeling fresh and bright.

WHITES

RIGHT: Nothing says beach better than interiors filled with a cool or pearly white backdrop paired with other muted tones. Consider white walls your easel. Art assumes greater prominence on a white backdrop. When a room, like this one, is filled with natural light, it makes sense to keep the mood bright with soft neutrals. This room riffs off the outdoor theme with a wood table, nature-inspired art, greenery, and accents in the colors of water and sand. Pops of blue inject a just-right visual break from the cocoon of white.

TURQUOISE

RIGHT: While blue is a standard seaside color, watery shades of turquoise are a familiar nod to coastal decor and appear frequently to keep the beachside ethos strong. Its many shades, hues, and tones conspire to create a world of happiness and harmony. The color is deeply ingrained in human history, from the Egyptians to Native Americans. It is believed that turquoise has spiritual healing powers so it's no surprise that the color brings feelings of tranquility and calm to any space.

The obvious allure of turquoise lies in that romantic image of white sandy beaches and blue waters. Turquoise, aquamarine, teal, and the many other variants work beautifully in an ocean-side decorating scheme. Including this favorite shade in a room is easily accomplished with a few accents like the chair, table, and art that bring a beachy feel to this corner. Turquoise is a color that combines the glitter of a jewel tone with the freshness of nature and the relaxation of an exotic getaway.

NEUTRALS

LEFT: Natural neutrals echo rolling dunes, sand, and driftwood, and provide harmony with nature while allowing textural elements to take center stage. The tranquil scheme provides welcome visual breaks, excellent backdrops, and restful moods. Here a light rug warms the wood floor while balancing the brightness created by the white fireplace and walls. A cluster of nature-themed accessories adds understated interest, as do a few blue accents that contribute a little dimension and also tie the space to its coastal roots.

BLUES

RIGHT: Blue is the lifeblood of the coast and its beloved shades come in as many moods as the sea and sky. With the soft blue of the walls and the view of the water as backdrops, this living room's furnishings embrace their surroundings. Several shades of blue work in chorus in spite of their diversity. By keeping the overall tone on the lighter side of the color and varying the patterns, the color palette doesn't fall flat, thanks to an abundance of fabrics that ensure continuity and cohesiveness while providing a soothing ambiance.

surfside embellishments

For a big impact with a coastal vibe and beachy flair, including iconic shore items is a must. Think surfboards, shells, starfish, sea glass, buoys, glass floats, and driftwood. They are the cornerstones of surfside style decor.

SURFBOARDS

Surfboards are the ultimate beach toys! When living surfside, what could be more fitting than including an iconic board inside or outside?

Surf culture is nothing new and its inclusion into interiors has become a design staple. Incorporating a surfboard in a room makes it feel simultaneously relaxed and put-together, adds a uniquely adventurous and fun-loving personality, and creates a focal point. Set outdoors, these legendary wave riders give any space an instant chill vibe.

BELOW: An orange board is a bright note in a sea of green. Its distinctive shape also contributes to the outdoor space by bringing an added dimension and balance to the slender shower.

ABOVE: Huddled under a palm tree next to a colorful little shack, a cheerful display of well-loved and much-used boards pays tribute to the nearby swells and their owner's love of the sport, while giving the space an undeniable cool vibe. As surfers know, it's always time to hang ten, and these boards are ready to ride at a moment's notice.

LEFT: The elegant lines, beautiful grain from balsa wood, and graphic design of this hand-shaped board make it a work of art perfectly suited to the simplicity of the space.

BELOW: Because of their size, surfboards are a notable addition to any room. This living room gets the perfect juxtaposition of boho and playfulness with a surfboard placed in a corner. It not only makes an impact, but it also pays homage to a free-spirited and relaxed lifestyle, and helps the room feel open and inviting.

SEASHELLS, STARFISH, CORAL, AND SEA GLASS

Seashells, starfish, and corals are naturally gorgeous. Their versatility makes them some of the most sought-after decor items to display the shore's beauty. Grouping shells together gives the impression of a well-curated collection, but even a single large one can become a focal point. Smaller ones can be used to hold an assortment of jewelry on a vanity, tea lights in any room, or keys in the entry. Whether you prefer to fashion shells and starfish into garlands and wind chimes, hang from chandeliers, frame a mirror, glue them on a fireplace mantel, or simply gather them in a glass bowl, the possibilities are endless, and all are sure to bring the magical bounty of the ocean inside.

ABOVE: Corals and shells of various sizes and shapes are unified by similar tone and graphic beauty. Arranging them on a shelf above a bank of windows overlooking the water harnesses the view and brings the coast indoors.

ABOVE: A collection of etchings and an ample display of spectacular shells integrate the vernacular of the coast in the design with originality and elegance.

ABOVE: The light streaming through this sculptural conch creates a luminescent effect that amplifies the shell's lustrous finish, gentle curves, and smooth texture. Its simple beauty and perfect pink hue make it a natural work of art.

ABOVE: Frosted, smooth sea glass takes many years to acquire its characteristic texture and shape. Rocky beaches and those with coarse sand yield beautiful specimens, especially during low tide and after a storm. Natural wood makes an organic companion for these opalescent treasures.

ABOVE: Massing sea glass in the same color family in a large bowl is a sure way to make a simple but impactful statement. The infinite variety of aqua hues—ranging from deep, light, and pale turquoise to greenish-blue undertones—complement each other and are further enhanced by the variety of shapes and sizes.

ABOVE: If you are a fan of crafting there are many ways to show off shapely starfish—from stringing them into a garland to attaching them to curtains, fireplaces, and more, but if you prefer a simple solution there is power in numbers as this cluster illustrates. Like their counterparts that illuminate the night skies, these enchanting sea creatures are truly the stars of the sea.

Sea glass comes from the broken shards of discarded bottles, shaped by time and the tides' persistent tumbling and turning until the shards' sharp edges are smoothed and rounded. During that long process the glass loses its lustrous surface but gains a frosted appearance. For beach walkers, there is no better moment than stumbling upon a piece of weather-worn, wave-battered glass. Sea glass inspires a palette of blues, greens, and opalescent whites.

BUOYS, GLASS FISHING FLOATS, AND DRIFTWOOD

Buoys are often used to mark the location of lobster traps. Originally, lobster buoys were created out of wood before they were painted using a number of colors. Today, most are made with Styrofoam but still bear bright colors. Lobster buoys have become something of a quintessential symbol of the New England coast, and as such are coveted by collectors. Vintage or new, these colorful floating devices reflect the romantic, rugged past of the world's oceans.

ABOVE TOP: Newly painted buoys sport numbers to identify a cottage and welcome visitors with their bright colors.

ABOVE: A simple shed goes from understated to cheerfully distinctive with colorful, weathered buoys hanging from its wall.

LEFT: A kaleidoscope of different-colored lobster buoys is one of the most beautiful and iconic images of Maine. Picturesque displays make for unique landscape art, hung on an outside shack or to mark the entrance to a beach house.

Glass fishing floats commonly come in round shapes and watery colors of blue and green, but can also appear in tube shapes and other hues like amber and purple. Though these orbs are no longer manufactured, authentic ones can still be found, and reproductions are readily available. Vintage or new, they are essential to shoreline vernacular.

LEFT: Glass floats are often associated with Japanese and Korean fishermen, but some vintage examples hail from Europe, Russia, and America. Contemporary versions, hand-blown by artisans, honor the originals. Their symmetry makes them ideal for display.

RIGHT: Gathered in a wooden crate, greenish-blue hydrangeas, white shells, and glass floats in colors ranging from clear to watery blues and greens bring nautical accents to a colorful coastal centerpiece.

Driftwood is one of nature's most wondrous creations. These treasures come in the form of washed-up bits of wood with their curious patterns and eroded forms.

Each piece of driftwood has its own journey and its own story. But its story isn't over when it washes up on the beach. Including driftwood in a space is not only a beautiful addition but also eco-friendly because the reclaimed old wood is used for creating new designs. The diversity of driftwood brings endless possibilities for artistic creations. When made into decorative pieces, these twisted branches, textures, and curves have another unique life.

ABOVE: Fitted with small votives, a gnarled, curvy driftwood branch in a natural finish brings the romance of the shore to the table.

LEFT: Pairing a sea-weathered, sun-bleached, salt-cured piece of driftwood coated in a subtle silvery wash with silky strands of found lobster warp creates a unique sculpture and an organic statement.

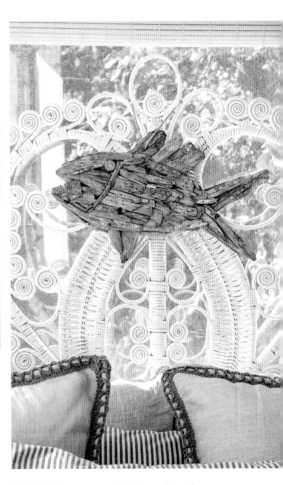

ABOVE: Wave-worn, naturally sculptural driftwood fashioned into a fish silhouette adds a whimsical coastal note to the wave-like design of a rattan headboard.

furnishings

Natural, enduring, textural, comfortable—these are the qualities that make time-honored coastal materials sure bets in a beach home.

Visual weight—or how the design elements look like they feel—is crucial. From beadboard to shiplap, wood, wicker, bamboo, roping, sisal, leather, nubby cotton and cushy pillows, hardy indoor-outdoor rugs, and a bit of a rough finish on wooden pieces invoke laid-back living. Painted items are also favored for their versatility. Modern pieces suit a contemporary look. Vintage furnishings evoke the past. Mixing the two together makes for an uncontrived interior. Light, moveable seating, such as floor cushions and footstools, are great to keep on hand. All-weather chairs in weather-resistant materials work beautifully inside and out.

ABOVE: Painting the whole room makes a great background for showing off soft furnishings and accessories. The open floor plan of this tiny beach cottage is all about simplicity, comfort, and convenience. The spool table makes a rustic counterpoint for the elegant slipcovered sofa. Striped chairs and curtains and a blue and white indoor-outdoor rug create an instant coastal look. Though the palette is pristine, everything is washable and child-friendly. The seaside location is made present with a shell chandelier, shore-related accessories, and pops of turquoise.

RIGHT: This living room showcases how eras, textures, patterns, and bright colors can successfully come together to create a space that is both energizing yet relaxing. Mid-century chairs take on an updated look when painted red. Their airy style balances the heft of the vintage coffee table, while the turquoise shutter lends a sense of history and is a pretty contrast to the chairs. Layering rugs provides not only comfort but also visual appeal. Select maritime accessories keep the seashore in soft focus.

ABOVE: Blues, neutrals, and the textural and organic elements of the furnishings confer a soothing mood and a gentle boho vibe to this restful bedroom.

ABOVE: The wicker chairs, ottoman, and the stone fireplace imbue this cozy space with classic good looks. The wood sign, shells, and corals nod to the beach location. The furnishings embrace contemporary and modern pieces in a way that subtly unites today and yesterday.

the homes

shack chic

LAGUNA, CA

Perched high on a bluff, Jimmy and Julia Hanna's historic cottage overlooks the Pacific Ocean and the beach that has always been Jimmy's favorite surf spot and where the couple became engaged.

"We are both from Laguna Beach and when the home came on the market, it was one of those things where we knew an opportunity like this was not going to come up again… oceanfront on our favorite beach? No way! We knew it was meant to be," Julia recalls. And so they bought the quintessential 1915 Laguna Beach surf shack. It was structurally sound, though Julia admits that, "It slopes more than we want and creaks a lot but we have gotten used to its quirkiness. However it was in dire need of aesthetic improvements." Julia turned to Tania Cassill of HUIT interior design and home furnishings boutique. Tania is known for creating beautiful, functional, environmentally conscious spaces." Tania and I had met

LEFT: For the breakfast room, which was part of a 1980s renovation that enclosed a deck, Tania decided to keep the rustic shingles in their original finish. "Since this area used to be the exterior, we thought we would keep its integrity and leave it natural," she explained. The window seat is made cozy with an assortment of cushions fashioned with vintage fabrics from HUIT. The Ilse Crawford-designed bamboo pendant light fixture and a round Saarinen-inspired pedestal, both from IKEA, team up with wicker chairs from All Modern, and a washable cotton rug (from HUIT) to convey a relaxed boho mood. For Tania, this is the coolest corner in the house. "You're literally almost cantilevered over the ocean," she says.

OVERLEAF: The deck's glass enclosure allows magnificent views of the coastline and the beach below. Modern teak lounge chairs are softened with cushy pillows. "Here all you need is a bathing suit and a good book, and when the surf is up you can just walk down to the water!" Julia says.

previously when my office was next door to her store," Julia says. "She came over to look at the house and even though this was in early June and I told her the work would need to be completed for the 4th of July, she said, 'Let's do it!'" True to her word, Tania completed the project in one month. "She totally beautified the house on the inside," Julia marvels. "For me, the biggest change came from painting the interior white. The original dark redwood paneling made the already tiny cottage feel even tinier, and the white immediately changed everything. I remember hesitating the day the painting was supposed to start because I was so afraid it would ruin the charm of the old walls, but after I saw that first coat of primer go up I was completely on board and couldn't wait to see the finished product, which was accomplished with Farrow & Ball All White and Benjamin Moore Simply White. It completely transformed the rooms into fresh, crisp spaces."

Julia shared a pinterest board with Tania so the designer could get a sense of the decor style she and Jimmy liked, "and then Tania did all of

FAR LEFT: Tania imbued the living room with casual beach elements that embrace the beauty of the coastal location. The end result is a light and fluid feel where comfort meets unpretentious style. Heaped with eclectic textile pillows from Tania's HUIT boutique, the IKEA sectional feels cocoon-like. The vintage seascape was a lucky local find. "The fireplace was original to the house, so I felt it was necessary to keep it authentic for the integrity of the home," Tania says. The built-in window seat offers additional seating and storage. The discreet sconce is from West Elm.

LEFT: An aqua vintage vase paired with glass beads from HUIT evoke the colors of the Pacific Ocean.

ABOVE: The newly painted original shiplap paneling frames the dining room windows and lets the view be the star. The black ceiling light pendant (from Cost Plus World Market) brings contrast to the white walls and adds a boho touch to the simple lines of the table and chairs. The wood of the original bookcase was in good condition but got a facelift with a coat of paint identical to the dining room walls.

RIGHT: When you live on the beach collecting sea glass is a must. Julia nestled her favorite green ones in an Abalone shell.

FAR RIGHT: A handmade frame surrounds a beach scene by photographer Gray Malin. Driftwood and plants bring nature indoors.

ABOVE: For the master bedroom Tania selected an upholstered linen bed frame that she dressed in white and blue bedding, including Bianca Leone pillows from HUIT. "I love the navy blue theme Tania incorporated," Julia says. "Something about it is very soothing and carries the colors of the water inside the house." A reclaimed wood bench from the designer's shop brings a rustic touch to the modern setting. The built-in storage was spruced up with elements from CB2.

LEFT: A Franco Albini ottoman nestles by a wicker chair to create a cozy reading nook. "I think every house should have something iconic," Tania says. The sunburst pillow (from HUIT) is one of Tania's favorites for its representative design. The Gray Malin photograph mirrors the local beach.

LEFT: The guest bedroom color scheme is a departure from the rest of the house because Julia wanted a fun and welcoming space for visiting family and friends. "The yellow bedding (from Paris, France) is so fresh and full of sunshine, perfect for a guest room," Tania says. The rattan chair, rug (both from HUIT), and colorful coastal-related framed prints add to the room's happy, easy-going mood. The one-of-a-kind DIY chandelier was made with materials from Cost Plus World Market and was cleverly executed by Tania.

her magic! Working with her was so easy!" she says. Today the boho chic interior speaks for itself. Julia's favorite spot is the breakfast room. "It has an entire 180-degree view of endless water, and on a clear day you can see Catalina Island in the distance. If I'm ever having a stressful day, I just watch people surf and it completely calms me down. In the evenings, we turn off all the lights in the house and the colors of the sunset fill the room. You feel like you're part of the sky. It's truly magical!" she says.

When it comes to decorating advice Julia is quick to say, "Hire Tania! I do mean that with my whole heart. But, if not Tania, then hire a designer like her, one who listens to you and works with you. You will gain a completely new perspective on things you never thought about and, hopefully, a friend!"

"I love the pillows Tania picked out. The colors and the patterns are slightly different but they all work together."

island vernacular

ANNA MARIA ISLAND, FL

Back in 1915 a barge transported a shack to this very spot on Anna Maria Island, a seven-mile narrow spit of land on Florida's Gulf Coast.

LEFT: The wood on the dining table evokes a casual beach-shack picnic table, while the metal base makes it current and practical. The knotted pendant light was chosen for its shade crafted of old crab traps and for its airy design that keeps the visual field unbroken, while adding a bit of structure that helps define the dining area. The bright orange chairs invigorate the space, while their molded plastic finish offers comfort and ease of upkeep.

The original owners enjoyed their summer days there for decades but also weathered many storms until the ramshackle cottage finally gave in to Mother Nature's harsh demands and was on the verge of crumbling. Enter architect Jody Beck of Tampa-based Traction Architecture to the rescue. However, what was intended to be a renovation turned into a rebuild.

PREVIOUS PAGE LEFT: Shiplap walls and galvanized steel cleats for drawer and cabinet pulls give the fully equipped kitchen a shipshape feel that fits into the open plan with ease. The island butcher block top and the bar stools add extra work space and seating to prepare and serve casual meals. The red barn-style pendants keep pace with the colors of the brilliant sunsets that can be enjoyed while cooking.

PREVIOUS PAGE RIGHT: The range also brings a burst of orange and is the kitchen's focal point. The quartz countertops and open shelves keep the overall look clean and simple.

LEFT: Waking up to the beckoning view of the sun-drenched beach is a lovely way to start the day. When nighttime comes, gentle breezes whispering through the trees and the soothing rhythm of the waves can't fail to lull you to a restful sleep.

BELOW: Whimsical signs spell out the famous laid-back lifestyle of the tropical island. The salvaged door pays homage to the original shack.

RIGHT: No self-respecting beachside home would be caught without a display of beach-found treasures. Here a lustrous pink conch glows in the sunlight.

PREVIOUS PAGES: In the main living space, glass doors lead to a wrap-around wood deck and the scene-stealing views of the beach and the Gulf of Mexico. Open trusses contribute an airy feeling while on the floor digitally printed porcelain tiles mimic wood planks, adding warmth and practicality. Modern furniture and pops of colors inspired by the sea and glorious Florida sunsets give the room its easy, upbeat comfort. Because storage and seating are always at a premium in smaller homes, a long bench was added to the back wall to provide both.

ABOVE: In keeping with the design of vernacular Florida cottages, the bedrooms and bathrooms are located directly off of the main living space. The sleeping loft's captain's ladder and built-in wood cabinetry nod to ship interiors. The built-ins are made of cypress, a wood species that is native to Florida and is resistant to termites and mold. The palm tree-inspired bead curtain conceals a small laundry room and the door to the bathroom.

The bright and airy beach house lures with its views and decorating scheme that create sensorial links with the water.

ABOVE: Pillows, towels, and hats are always on standby for a day at the beach. A map shows the original plots of the island. Items gathered on the shelf speak of travels near and far.

"The original house had deteriorated over the years and was in very poor shape structurally. It also was not elevated, so it was vulnerable to flooding during hurricane season. Strict storm codes made a rehab nearly impossible," the architect says. The difficult decision to take it down and rebuild had to be made.

Anything that could be saved from the derelict cottage, like the interior doors, was reused in the new house to keep the memories of the bygone shack alive. The goal was to design a space that would fit in with the smaller-scale Old Florida-style beach bungalows, and honor

their heritage. Today the 1,200 square-foot cottage is a modern version of its old self. "We looked at lots of beach bungalows and Florida Cracker cottages for inspiration," the architect says. In the end, she replicated the original cottage's exact same floor plan, down to the placement of windows. She calls the new home a modern interpretation of an elevated beach bungalow. "It feels like Old Florida still," she says, "but it's safe and protected."

Along with its dreamy location and a mere 75 steps to the soft, warm sand of the shore, Mark and Rosa Heller's bright and airy beach house lures with its views and decorating scheme that create sensorial links with the water.

The breezy rooms feature forms, furniture, and accents that echo the qualities of life on the island. With its soaring ceiling, comfy furnishings in shades of oranges, blues, and greens, and unobstructed views of the Gulf of Mexico the living room's open concept instantly invites both fun and rest. The brilliant, joyful color scheme carries on throughout the open kitchen, dining area, and bedrooms, as does the overall relaxed mood that Mark and Rosa fittingly call "chic boho coastal". They love being able to share their unique cottage with friends and guests. The beach, beautiful surroundings, and close proximity to the local village also make it a prime candidate for vacation stays.

LEFT: At ground level, a small but efficient patio is home to a porch swing and outdoor shower, both painted in Navel by Sherwin-Williams, and storage space for surfboards, bicycles, kayaks, and paddleboards.

ABOVE: Surf's up! Who could resist riding the waves, especially when you live right on the beach and the water is so inviting!

ABOVE: Wicker armchairs were replaced with an upholstered pair Lisa had in her office. "I loved Gayle's style and wanted to keep the beachy feel but have it be a little less literal and a touch more structured, while still being comfortable," she explains. The curtains, oars, and the wood fish at the entrance to the kitchen stayed with the cottage, but the California sign is one the family picked up on a spontaneous trip. "It was a magical time. It reminds us not to overthink things," she says.

RIGHT: Lisa kept the couch but changed the slipcover, and added neutral pillows with muted navy stripes. The painted spool table came with the cottage. The shell chandelier is Lisa's favorite new addition to the room. "I liked the idea of adding something large as a statement piece," she says. "It's often the first thing people see when they walk in and it lets you know we can all be fabulous at the beach even with our flip flops and floppy hats!" She swapped all of the window shades to new ones in a flax color. "They used to be darker and some were bamboo. I wanted smoother transitions from one color to the next and consistency from one window to the other."

tiny haven

CAPE COD, MA

A few years ago while spending a Labor Day weekend in Dennis Port, MA, Lisa Hicks, her husband Ken, and their four young children Naia, Ellery, Emmeline, and Simon, fell in love with the charming, seasonal seaside community.

"We had been looking for a second home for quite sometime but always got cold feet when we thought about maintenance," Lisa says. But, as fate would have it, a sweet, tiny cottage came up for sale. Lisa and Ken met with Rob and Gayle Macchi who had owned the little gem for several years and had already made all the major improvements. "We spent six memorable summers making this beach bungalow our very own," Gayle says.

FOOTPRINTS IN THE SAND

"I have a natural attraction to this color palette, and love the colors of the water and the beach, so I was thrilled to have a space that I could infuse with my love for the ocean."

"We brought the cottage down to the original studs and ripped up the old carpet and linoleum flooring." Rob also built the loft and ladder, incorporated the front porch into a sleeping porch, added new pine flooring, put a large picture window in the living area, and opened up the kitchen by removing the window over the sink, upgraded the appliances with new stainless steel, and, finally, the couple painted all the dark pine white, including walls, ceilings, floors, and beams. The Macchis had accomplished not only these extensive renovations but they also decorated the space in such a fresh and charming style that Lisa, herself

ABOVE LEFT AND RIGHT: Lisa got a new white velvet headboard (Birch Lane), bed spread (Pine Cone Hill), comforter (Piper Classics), striped pillow from a shop in Harwichport, MA, and a large indoor/outdoor rug made from recycled materials, but kept the pendant lamps that came with the cottage. The loft is 12-year-old Naia's favorite sleeping and reading place. The black oar, sailboat, the Footprints in the Sand sign, and the rattan trunk are pieces from the previous owners.

an interior designer, and Ken were smitten, and purchased the 1930s Nantucket Sound cottage with all the furnishings.

That was in 2017 and although Lisa has kept most of the Macchis' decor, she has been slowly but surely adding her own touches. "We were thrilled to be lucky to find a space that was visually appealing from the day we moved in. I loved walking in and having it feel finished," she explains. "But I have found it challenging to make decorating changes out of respect for Rob and Gayle. We wanted to honor their legacy." It was only this past summer that she began to question, "If this were a blank canvas what would I do?" And then granting herself permission to start making the changes that, she says, "will truly make the cottage ours."

However, it's a work in progress as the couple gradually find things to replace some of the beautiful pieces that were already there with new ones that truly speak to their entire family.

ABOVE: Lisa kept the curtains and shutters of the little opening connecting the bed area to the space previously added by Rob, now used for the bunk beds.

OVERLEAF LEFT: Ken built the bunk beds right inside the little space adjoining the bedroom so they would fit perfectly, and made the rope ladder from supplies he purchased at a boat store nearby. Ten-year-old Ellery sleeps on the top bunk. "In the mornings she will peak her head through to say good morning!" Lisa says. "The bottom bed provides an extra spot for the kids' overnight guests, which happens often."

The quaint and breezy beach retreat is the perfect little getaway from the bustling city. Lisa loves light colors, especially in this small space. "It opens it up so much! When I walk in and see the soft furnishings, elegant lines, and select elements that bring the outside in it allows me to exhale, relax, and reset." But equally important she adds, "We also knew it would bring an 'old school' childhood to our kids with all the precious summer memories that come with it. It is such a unique, friendly community. It feels like family."

ABOVE RIGHT: Ellery saw this pillow at HomeGoods on Cape Cod and had to have it! "She loved the sparkles and I thought it was the perfect inspiration piece to help create a little girl space where she could blossom," Lisa recalls.

RIGHT: Water sports abound in the area. "One of the first things our kids did after we purchased the cottage was run outside and count the steps to the beach." Lisa says. "They were thrilled to announce '100 steps!'" The mirror used to be on the front porch but Lisa moved it to this wall to help open the space up by adding more reflection, and painted it Ocean Air by Benjamin Moore.

PREVIOUS PAGE LEFT: "There are six of us and two dogs co-existing in this little cottage. I love it because it means that our family is close together, which brings new lessons about respect and compassion for each of us," Lisa reflects. "We also had to learn to live a more minimal lifestyle with fewer things." White rollup shades at the windows make the sleeping porch an airy bedroom. The simple but comfy space is Emmeline and her brother Simon's sleeping quarters.

PREVIOUS PAGE TOP LEFT: As with the rest of the cottage, Ken and Lisa gave every room several coats of white paint. One of two twin beds nestles into a just-right space around the corner. The little shutters were refreshed with Ocean Air by Benjamin Moore, and Lisa had the "Beach" sign custom made.

PREVIOUS PAGE TOP RIGHT: The changes Lisa and Ken made to the kitchen are mostly cosmetic. They sanded the countertop, stained it in a driftwood finish, and painted the trim with Ocean Air. They added the "Gather" sign above the windows, a rug, and aqua mason jars. The chandelier, McKenzie Child cabinet hardware, and the appliances came with the cottage.

PREVIOUS PAGE BOTTOM LEFT: Lisa had been eyeing the rattan peacock headboard for a while and knew this was the perfect spot for it. "It is one of my favorite things," she says. "It is so soft and pretty and allows the light from the window to shine through, but it also provides structure to the bed." The driftwood fish adds a fun touch.

PREVIOUS PAGE BOTTOM RIGHT: With storage at a premium the Macchis had installed hooks and pegs all around the house, providing function but also charm to hold clothing, towels, and more. Lisa kept this clever wood-and-twine rack with hooks for kitchenware.

RIGHT: The Hicks family lives large in their tiny 500 square-feet summer getaway in Dennis Port. "This seasonal (May to October) cottage community is so charming and friendly," Lisa says. "Here our kids can safely play outside with their friends, swim, bike, and, well, just be kids! By night we often have communal dinners with our neighbors. This is a unique family community."

seaside zen

SANTA BARBARA, CA

Santa Barbara designer Jodi Goldberg of Jodi G Designs is known for her organic interiors and her tried-and-true philosophy.

"When I design for my clients, the first step is to get to know how they want to live in their spaces," she explains. "I want to make each room functional, with a specific intention in mind, and create the magic to bring their vision to life." That individual and sensitive approach results in spaces that are both meaningful and personal.

LEFT: The lush plantings surrounding the home provides understated exotic touches that soften the deck's new metal railing that was added to give the traditional craftsman bungalow a little bit of a modern upgrade.

RIGHT: A former driveway was reconfigured to make room for a bohemian-inspired outdoor living space. A dense bamboo hedge shelters the intimate setting that welcomes with organic textures and warm blue hues. The sofa cushions are made from a replica of a vintage Batik fabric from Indonesia while the decorative pillows are finished with authentic material from the Hmong villages on the border of China and Vietnam.

When Jodi was asked to reinvent a classic 1920s beach home on a quaint ocean-view property in Santa Barbara's storybook "Bungalows," she aimed for the harmony and serenity her client was seeking. Home to a single mother and her young daughter, the 1,300-square-foot craftsman bungalow offered the perfect size for the duo but was in need of a major overhaul, including gutting the kitchen, floors, and even the closets. "The biggest challenges were construction and timing. All the work had to be completed and all the brand new furniture in place in less than four months," Jodi says. "We definitely were out of our client's comfort zone

ABOVE: A serene palette, ethnic prints, and exotic objects bring an air of bohemian sophistication and a spiritual vibe to the light-filled living room. The neutral scheme is enhanced with the textures and materials from thoughtfully curated pieces, including a sofa covered with sustainable fabric, cotton ottomans, and eco-friendly armchairs that embody boho chic, a tactile nubby rug, a mirror from Bali, and an organic driftwood floor lamp. A pensive Buddha presides on a coffee table that was found locally.

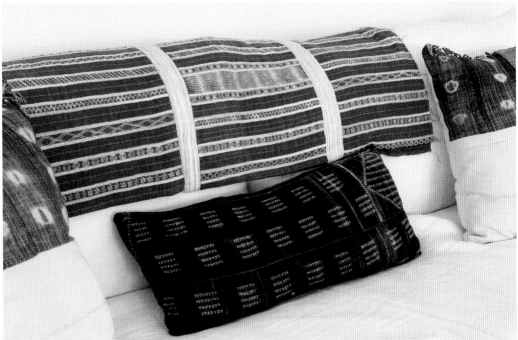

ABOVE TOP: The fireplace underwent a facelift with paint and a mantel made from reclaimed wood from an old barn. Coral and driftwood perpetuate the simple but organic feel.

ABOVE: Made with Indonesian batik and African mudcloth, the indigo pillows and throw contribute exotic layers and enliven the otherwise subdued palette of the room.

ABOVE: The dining room is adjacent to the living room so keeping the color scheme and decor consistent was part of the overall design concept. Jodi sourced a table made with acacia wood from Indonesia and covered the custom Palecek end chairs with batik from Bali. The four wicker chairs have an organic elegance. In the corner, a little wooden stool painted white strikes a whimsical note. The built-in shelves were custom made to replace the original ones that had fallen apart. "Built-ins are the best thing in small houses," Jodi says. "And don't be afraid to mix new and reclaimed woods." A grouping of African vintage baskets brings more textural touches. The glass beads beneath the hemp-wrapped frame of the chandelier bring shimmer and make a romantic statement.

TOP RIGHT: Jodi chose the vase for its shape and pattern representative of a modern take on a seashell.

BOTTOM RIGHT: Moroccan tiles inspired by the forms, patterns, and lines created by the unique process of shibori bring the ancient Japanese form of textile dyeing to the buffet.

as far as style and even hiring a designer. We worked very well with her and it was a lovely experience."

Inspired by her client's warmth and natural inclination toward the California esthetic, Jodi set out to create a soothing interior infused with a quiet boho vibe.

The Zen ambiance of the rooms comes from a mix of subtle white, neutrals, and earth tones enhanced by organic textures, the intrigue of modern pieces, cool blue accents, and raw wood. In the family-focused home, classic elements coexist harmoniously with non-traditional ones and encourage peaceful relaxation, while being able to withstand kids coming and going.

Jodi and her team worked closely with the owner to envision a space that was both modern and fresh while still retaining a sense of character, narrative, and individual personality. Today the little boho beach bungalow's aura radiates with a calming energy and soulful beauty.

ABOVE LEFT: Together, an oak vanity, a mirror, a carved-wood medallion, and a little boho stool bring a new and modern attitude to the small bathroom.

ABOVE CENTER: Greenery from the garden, sea glass from the beach, and healing crystals conspire to bring the benefit of nature indoors.

ABOVE RIGHT: The nightstand with delicate mother-of-pearl inlay nods to far away cultures. Its size is just right for displaying favorite books and items, like the Surf sign from Meadow Rose Photography and vintage bottles with sea-inspired finials.

RIGHT: Shades of blues and creams make the bedroom an oasis of calm. The carved-wood bed dressed with Vietnamese pillows in diverse patterns and a striped cotton throw invites restful sleep. The reclaimed wood bench and a small table with a marble top contribute layers of rusticity. The chandelier's canopy echoes the neutral tone of the natural grass weave of the window shades.

coastal vibes

LIDO BEACH, FL

Life has an unexpected way of putting people together. Dale Rieke, an Ohio native, and Jenny Acheson, born in Zambia, met at a surf and yoga camp in Costa Rica.

Though from different parts of the world they shared a love of travel, which for Dale means indulging his love of surfing and, for Jenny, pursuing her photography career. Eventually the pair found their way to Florida. In 2012, during the week they decided to get married, they came across their beach house. "Dale had been coming to Lido Beach since he was 12 so it made sense when we found the house. He and I are free-spirited types and threw ourselves wholeheartedly into creating our Lido Beach House," Jenny recalls. One could say it was a match made in heaven: Dale is not only an accomplished surfer but also a skilled craftsman who has been designing and building furniture for 30 years.

the sun-kissed beach house captures the essence of tropical bliss.

PREVIOUS PAGE TOP LEFT: The minute the waves are up, Dale is ready to grab one of his many surfboards depending on the conditions. "Long board for small waves, short one for bigger waves," Jenny says. The location also lends itself to bike rides among the cottages, gardens, and shops, along paths lined with tropical trees and fragrant exotic plants. When the original Lido sign fell apart Dale created a new one. "The previous one was made with old '50s shop lettering," Jenny recalls. "We painted the new wood ones the same colors as the former ones."

PREVIOUS PAGE BOTTOM LEFT: A grouping of '50s spun fiberglass furniture clearly communicates the era's design style. The settee's weatherproof cushions sport a colorful tropical design befitting the location.

PREVIOUS PAGE CENTER: Perfect for just hanging around or to enjoy a relaxing little siesta, a hammock from Panama nestles among the verdant foliage of sea grape hedges.

PREVIOUS PAGE RIGHT: Dale constructed the bougainvillea-draped arbor, sign, and walkway several years ago. Jenny points out that a new arbor is in the works as this one has weathered over the years.

"Our style leans toward mid-century but with eclectic, colorful, and global additions."

"It is a wonderful space for Dale to showcase his talent as a furniture designer and builder. He draws on many years of experience in order to renovate with great care and not cut corners," Jenny says. Herself an accomplished photographer, Jenny found an innovative way to display her work and worldly goods and embark on a new field of interest. "The project provided a venue to share art and treasures from our voyages, and to discover my taste for design and decorating," she says. "Buying furniture at auctions was an exciting pastime, knowing we could easily fix up an old Paul McCobb table or a Herman Miller chair if needed."

However, it took a lot of work and determination to transform the interior of the 1960s home into the haven it is today.

"It was furnished but in a terribly dated shabby beach style. We thought we could keep it as is for a while but after a few days we just gave it all away to charitable organizations," Jenny says. "We already had a lot of furniture from auctions and from an apartment I had in New York and Dale went ahead with the renovations."

ABOVE: Nature plays an indirect but major role in the living room decor. On one side, matured birds of paradise align like a live sculpture while on the other side bamboos and palms create a jungle-like tableau. Together with the terrazzo floor, a new birch wood wall built by Dale contributes to the sleek beauty of the room. "I am attracted to eclectic decorating influences but with a strong, simple starting point," Jenny says. "The sofa hails from California and the mid-century chairs and bamboo stool were scored at an auction. The teak table rests on a Persian rug which once belonged to my mother."

LEFT: For pillows, like these ones, Jenny shops from Shine Shine in Cape Town, South Africa. "I also bought blankets, tin trays, and lots of other cool accessories from the shop," she says. The globe reflects the couple's love of travel.

LEFT: The remodeled kitchen boasts birch walls, cabinets, and shelves all built by Dale, who also made the small decorative surfboard to hold the Lido Beach House business cards. The framed surfboard photo is by Jenny. It is glued on wood. The ceiling light fixture was an auction find. Yellow metal stools and bright green and orange accessories are proof of Jenny's design mantra: "I like bright colors usually but with a clean, painted background, and I'm not afraid of things clashing."

TOP RIGHT: Though disparate in their designs, the blankets from Shine Shine have color and texture in common. The lamp on the side table is originally from India but Jenny bought it at Urban Outfitters. The Cuba poster, an auction purchase, makes a fitting companion to Dale's wall. The decorative wood surfboard Dale made 10 years ago embodies his love of the sport and his masterful woodworking skills.

BOTTOM RIGHT: Dale's woodworking magic is evident not only in the wall but also in the precision with which he designed and built the headboard. "Our beach house would not exist if not for Dale's expertise in renovating," Jenny explains. "He has an excellent sense of scale and design. We have similar tastes though he would probably be more minimal if it wasn't for me!" Jenny got the quilt and blanket from Shine Shine.

"I am attracted to eclectic decorating influences but with a strong simple starting point."

The location leant itself to beachy decor but apart from the surf theme running through the house, Dale and Jenny kept away from the typical shell motifs, pastel colors, and overstuffed furniture.

"Our style leans towards mid-century but with eclectic, colorful, and global additions. I gravitate to anything that has good design, whether it is an African papier-mâché bowl or the clean lines of a modern piece of furniture. I have been a collector of many things—Queen Elizabeth biscuit tins and mugs, African fabric, '60s ceramics, artwork, photography, Turkish and Persian rugs, etc.—and have gathered over the years rather than made multiple purchases to furnish places." Without a doubt the couple's home is an expression of their style.

And though it is packed with personal art, treasures, and Dale's furniture, they are happy to share it with guests looking for a sun-kissed beach house that captures the essence of tropical bliss.

free spirit

ENCINITAS, CA

Encinitas, California has long drawn surfers with its unique and dynamic blend of top surf shops, not to mention its beaches coveted by locals as hidden gems.

The beaches include Swami, a favorite surfing spot immortalized in the song "Surfin' USA" by the Beach Boys, Moonlight State Beach, and D Street Beach where surfers ride in on long rolling waves. The magnetic pull of the coastal town proved irresistible to Nikki and Steve Carlson, and D Street is where they found their 1930s cottage and its little studio, which they dubbed Cottage + Sea. "We actually decided on the name a day before we found our home because our dream was to find an old cottage with personality and we knew we wanted to be close to the sea for its active and relaxed lifestyle. When we found the property, we knew it was for us," Nikki says. "We loved its character and charm." Steve is an avid surfer and he and Nikki share a love of the laid-back boho surf life.

But when the young couple bought their newfound nest they had to update pretty much everything, but making sure to do so in a way that would preserve its original style.

LEFT: The living room is all about softness and textures. "Soothing neutrals feel like a breath of fresh air and an extension of the white sandy beaches," says Nikki, who brought in the warm textures of the cane sofa (from CB2) and rattan chairs (from World Market) to provide balance. "We like to layer patterns to make spaces cozy and welcoming," she adds. "We favor small business makers and shop locally as much as possible." The pillows came from several sources including local and online shops, among which are The Life Styled Home in Encinitas, Kaekoo Shop, The Loomia, Kip and Co, and The Home Mind. A Turkish rug from Pottery Barn and a throw from Olive & Linen heighten the comfort quotient. No surfer would ignore the good Karma of finding a discarded board! "This one was left in our yard," Nikki says. "It had a vintage feel so we cleaned it up and it fits perfectly within our home's history."

LEFT: The guest studio is all about comfort, charm, and convenience. The kitchen offers all the expected amenities while the wood-like tiles provide easy maintenance and durability. Atop the island a live-edge wood shelf brings in an organic element while the blue globes speak of the ocean.

ABOVE: In decorating the sleeping area Nikki's goal was to create a fun and relaxing space: "We love white and natural pieces that bring the outdoors inside with pops of wood and plants. Pillows from Kaekoo Shop, a blanket from Dynamikos, and a print from local photographer Alex Clark of Salty Gloss add light-hearted boho touches.

RIGHT: "Before we made the updates, the bathroom was entirely green (including the tub) and didn't have a separate shower so we opened through to the closet in the adjacent room to allow for individual spaces," Nikki recalls. To create a serene spa-like mood they opted to go with white walls and fixtures. "We wanted the room to make a peaceful statement. The white scheme and just enough touches of wood create a calm and restful oasis." Rather than hampering the natural light coming from the window, a delicate rattan light pendant allows it to spill through.

After completing many renovation projects came the fun part: decorating. Uniting coziness and function was high on the couple's priority list. "We believe that functionality is paramount, and then the design components follow," Nikki says. "We live so close to the beach that including elements like rattan furniture, plants, and surfboards was natural."

The end result is a harmonious blend of mid-century modern, Scandinavian, and Moroccan influences, with just the right touch of sophistication. In furnishing their home they agree that gathering items over time works best. "We love finding things that spark joy and fit perfectly in our space so we are always willing to wait until we find the right piece, and then it is always much more meaningful," Nikki notes. A neutral palette sets a quiet mood and welcomes hints of greens through plants and blues that allude to the near-by ocean. "We have limited space and we don't want rooms to become cluttered so the biggest challenge is refraining from getting everything we love. If we get something new, we eliminate something else. We like living minimally."

Steve and Nikki prefer one-of-a-kind items, handmade pieces from local shops, and those passed on from generations. "They carry so much love and meaning," Nikki says. She also believes in decorating from your heart and soul, and with thoughtfulness. "Never try to conform to someone else's style," she advises. "Go with what makes you feel good, playful, and relaxed. Create that 'aloha spirit' and have fun doing it." Steve and Nikki's design philosophy accomplishes just that. It is a true reflection of their personalities, and a love letter to their home and lifestyle.

"We love finding things that spark joy and fit perfectly in our space."

"Go with what makes you feel good, playful, and relaxed. Create that 'aloha spirit' and have fun doing it."

LEFT AND BELOW: On the back patio no-fuss furnishings (from Target) are designed to hold up in all weather conditions. The center pit is filled with blue glass to mimic the ocean. Plumerias contribute a lush background and cast their sweet fragrance far and wide.

Nikki affectionately calls this area the "surf hub." "Steve owns a number of surfboards for various surfing conditions," she explains. "One in particular, Rusty Dozer, is just right for spots he likes to surf at, like D Street Beach, which is just a stone's throw from our home."

"This fire pit is a great focal point," Nikki says. "We love to promote the community aloha spirit and have people over for drinks or to barbecue, and this is the perfect spot."

ABOVE LEFT AND RIGHT: Nikki says that the idea for the front patio was to bring the indoor outside and have a cozy setting for entertaining or just relaxing. The teak sofa with water-resistant cushions (from Wayfair) and rattan-look-alike chairs (from Target) are stylish yet durable. An umbrella (from World Market), pillows, and fragrant Plumeria blossoms add to the inviting setting. "This fire pit is a great focal point," Nikki says. "We love to promote the community aloha spirit and have people over for drinks or to barbecue, and this is the perfect spot."

LEFT: In the living room a soothing palette delivers calming tones, while furnishings and art provide beauty and comfort in equal measure. A cushy sectional upholstered in Belgian linen, and a coffee table crafted from salvaged elm, contribute to the organic mood.

serene sensibility

SANTA BARBARA, CA

While on a vacation, Elizabeth Burns and her family drove from San Francisco to San Diego. "I fell in love with Santa Barbara and knew it was where I was meant to be," Elizabeth says.

"Our daughter had also decided to go to college in California so I bit the bullet and rented a condo while I searched for a house." Nine months later she found it. "I hadn't set out looking for a modern home. But as soon as I stepped inside and saw the curtains blowing through the open French doors, the light, the views of the ocean and gorgeous mountains… I was smitten!" Elizabeth recalls. "I called my husband on the East Coast and told him this was the one. It had just come on the market and we bought it that day."

ABOVE: Next to a modern chair, a rustic little table illustrates Elizabeth's affinity for including an antique piece in each room, while elements borrowed from nature carry on the organic theme.

RIGHT: "I knew I would need storage and this replica of a printer's chest of drawers was one of the first pieces I bought for the house," Elizabeth recalls. "It holds everything from table linens to candles, giftwrapping supplies, and board games." It also offers a staging area for seasonal displays.

TOP FAR RIGHT: Elizabeth, who began her career as a watercolor artist, turned the back wall into a gallery to showcase her extensive collection of seascapes. "I actually bought the first painting more than 20 years ago when I still lived in Connecticut," she says. "Once I moved to Santa Barbara, I started collecting in earnest. Many of the pieces are from Mate Gallery (including the huge basket), some are gifts, and a few are my own, and all together they form a collection of things I treasure."

BOTTOM FAR RIGHT: Elizabeth is partial to singular color groupings, like the blue sea glass simply displayed on the coffee table. "They tie in with my color palette," she says.

OVERLEAF LEFT: "I love the feel of walking through our front door and seeing how the house completely opens up with the ceilings peaking at 12 feet," Elizabeth says. "Although not a large home, the high ceilings and the sheer quantity of glass allow this house to live larger than it is." The ample salvaged pine table instills an earthy note. "I wanted something casual and not too precious that friends and family could gather around," Elizabeth explains. With its tiny heart cutouts, a wood screen from Indonesia adds a sentimental touch and a gentle hint of color.

OVERLEAF RIGHT: In the dining room the connection to the outdoors is evident. A bank of sliding doors opens onto a terrace. Outfitted with all the comforts needed, it is equally used for quiet meals and entertaining. On the indoor dining table a wooden dough bowl holds some of Elizabeth's sea glass collection. "There is something calming about living by the water. One of my favorite pastimes is taking long walks on the beach and hunting for sea glass," she says.

"One of my favorite pastimes is taking long walks on the beach, and hunting for sea glass."

LEFT: A den adjacent to the kitchen welcomes with its fireplace and comfy chairs. On the mantel an African basket coexists with vintage French bottles, a match striker—a souvenir from Vermont—and a little wooden house Elizabeth fell in love with. "The kitchen's original wood cabinets had turned orange in color, and the floor was black linoleum, which made the space one of the darker places in the house," Elizabeth says. "We painted everything white, added the skylight, and replaced the linoleum with engineered oak. It completely changed the look of the room." Vintage canisters from Mate Gallery, a favorite Santa Barbara shop, perfectly match the aqua subway tiles and, together with rustic wooden bowls, temper the modernity of the room.

ABOVE AND LEFT: Elizabeth also found the rope-wrapped decorative surfboard at Mate Gallery. Its organic texture, color, shape, and height proved to be the perfect complement for the inviting corner. The wool pouf from CB2 is easily moved as an extra seat or a place to prop your feet up. "I've become a fan of blue and smatter it about during the warmer months," Elizabeth says. "I found the handmade throw in Vermont and the pillow is one of many I have bought from Patine in Santa Cruz. I love the nubby texture and simple stripe."

"I enjoy mixing materials and styles. If I love something, I find a way to make it work."

One of the many features Elizabeth loves about her home is the abundance of natural light and the connection to the outdoors through seven sets of French doors and multiple windows. "Because of that, and the fact that it's under 2,000-square-feet, we call the it 'The Little Glass House,'" she says fondly.

Elizabeth was seduced not only by the house but by the California lifestyle as well, and both played a starring role in the evolution of her career.

"I've always been interested in design, from staging to consulting and styling, but when I moved here from Connecticut I stumbled upon Porch, a wonderful Santa Barbara home and garden shop with a captivating organic feeling. I instantly knew that was the way I wanted my own home to feel," she explains. "Our mid-century modern house became my canvas for trying new things and experimenting, and this is where my company, edb Designs, began."

Offering an effortless feeling of space and flow, where organic meets coastal esthetic and sophistication, Elizabeth's home radiates a stylish simplicity and beautiful functionality. "It's all about the connection to

RIGHT: The master bedroom's neutral palette exudes serenity. Elizabeth chose materials, subtle color accents, and greenery to keep the space from looking cold. The muted pillows bring a gentle influx of texture to the linen bed. Wood stools warm up cool, metal black tables, while over the bed the round shape of a vintage basket softens the ceiling lines. The intricate wall hanging is a work of art in its own right. The weathered paint of the vintage trunk also helps keep the room grounded.

BOTTOM LEFT: Coral, starfish, and greenery conjure up the nearby ocean and surrounding nature.

BOTTOM RIGHT: The bowl's patina makes the perfect foil for abalone shells Elizabeth picked up on a rocky beach.

RIGHT: Using a few but significant components, Elizabeth created an inspiring Zen tableau with a unity of colors and textures. A wooden vase and bowl from Africa respectively hold elegant leaves from her garden and green sea glass. A stack of small stones brings to mind the calming ritual that comes with balancing them.

LEFT: The guest bedroom unites old and new. Rustic items like the ladder and bench balance the modern bed and tables. A macramé wall hanging from Bangladesh, a woven basket, and furry pillows inject boho touches. "I enjoy mixing materials and styles," Elizabeth explains. "If I love something, I find a way to make it work."

ABOVE LEFT: White sea glass and smooth wood appear to be made for each other.

ABOVE RIGHT: Elizabeth purchased the painting of Big Sur from her Instagram friend, Tara Weilbacher, who gifted her with the little painting of the trees on the other side of the bed. "I love our Instagram community!" she exclaims.

OVERLEAF LEFT: A variety of bamboos add to the appeal of the outdoor shower. "I love showering outdoors in the sunshine, especially after a beach walk. This was a must for me," Elizabeth says. "I designed it so that it would be simple with only one knob. I wanted it to blend into the landscape. The deck is made of ipe wood, a beautiful, exotic Brazilian walnut." Elizabeth's daughter Kelsey is the surfer in the family. "After she bought the surfboard she realized it wouldn't fit in her apartment so we keep it for her," Elizabeth explains. "Orange is way outside my color palette, but once I found a place for it in the garden I loved it!"

OVERLEAF RIGHT: "My husband Kevin was instrumental in getting the backyard project under way," Elizabeth says. "I've always done my own outdoor spaces but knew we needed help with this one. The previous owners never used the backyard. It was just a rectangle of grass so we started from scratch. We actually enlarged it, added new landscaping, a custom-built gas fire pit, a redwood hot tub, and of course the outdoor shower!" Now a wall composed of local stones and concrete pavers define the back patio where teak and concrete furniture gathers around the fire pit to form a cozy outdoor living room. "It's an awesome place for parties," Elizabeth says. "After dinner we retire here for a fire and dessert...or sometimes we have cocktails and watch the sun turn the mountains pink."

nature and blurring the lines between inside and out," she observes. "I am all in favor of accentuating the light quality. I like a calm, serene feeling in my home. The challenge was how to keep a mid-century modern home from feeling cold and unwelcoming. It is made up of glass, metal, and stucco, which aren't exactly warm materials. I also love antiques and wanted to incorporate some that wouldn't feel out of place."

To meet her goal Elizabeth started with a neutral foundation, furnishings with clean lines, and then layered textures, meaningful accessories, art, and plants to bring the rooms to life. "A home has to have a soul," she says. "It can be from a quirky piece found on a trip, art, local treasures like a collection of sea glass, or an antique piece that speaks to me. I always include a natural element may it be driftwood or shells and something old or vintage in every space." Elizabeth's Little Glass House not only has a soul but it is also a breath of fresh air.

LEFT: "In classic shingle-style architecture, the incorporation of positive and negative space is key!" Sandra explains. "We love this porch because it gets the southwest summer breeze, while protecting us from the sun. The view is beautiful and the peacefulness from the rhythm of the waves is ever so soothing." A mix of furnishings collected from local shops and flea markets stands up to the weather.

seaworthy sanctuary

CAPE COD, MA

When Sandra and Phil Cavallo bought an abandoned 1905 Folk Victorian home on a bluff overlooking Old Silver Beach in Cape Cod's West Falmouth, their intention was to refurb it.

"We had fallen in love with the simple details of the house— West Falmouth pink granite in the foundation from the historic West Falmouth quarry, circa 1800s, the arched entry to the covered porch, the character of the old doors, the original trim work, and the beach-rock fireplace," Sandra recalls. "Unfortunately the house was too far gone. We carefully disassembled it piece by piece down to the deck, leaving only the original beach rock fireplace and chimney, saving all we could reuse in the building of the new home."

For inspiration, the couple turned to the turn-of-the-century beach "cottages," that lined the New England coast. "We researched shingle-style architecture, and drove up and down the shore taking pictures, noticing important features of those period seaside homes," Sandra recounts.

FAR LEFT: The side entry is a perfect spot to keep water sports equipment on hand. Phil is a wind-junky and Buzzards Bay is famous for its wind. "He, and our twins, Gianni and Nathalie, use this board to surf on while they have a harness around their waist, which clips into a large arc-shaped kite—the kite carries them across the water!" Sandra says.

LEFT: Concrete seagulls were once used as decoys to deter predatory birds from taking over nests. These replicas make a fitting metaphor for a family home.

ABOVE: In Japan, for centuries spherical glass fishing floats served the same purposes as foam or wooden buoys—marking a community's lobster spots and fishing lines in the open sea. Currents carried them across the seas. Vintage or new, these legendary orbs work beautifully as classic coastal accessories on any shore.

RIGHT AND FAR RIGHT: Constructed from mahogany wood, the double outdoor showers were designed to comfortably accommodate the Cavallos' many summer guests. "Everyone is back and forth to the beach all day and having two showers allows for us all to rinse the sand off comfortably," Sandra says.

After interviewing a few local architects she realized she couldn't get exactly what she was after design-wise. So she took matters into her own hands and drew on the knowledge she had gained from studying at the famed School of Visual Arts NYC and, subsequently, from her years designing products for licensed companies. She and Phil sat at a local bar one night and Sandra sketched the house on a paper placemat. "We took it to a draftswoman and she re-sketched it perfectly. We asked her to draw the plans," Sandra explains. Once the house was built, Sandra set out to furnish it. "Whether it's layers of elaborate interest or simple modern spaces, I like it visually clean and prefer a collected home to

"I love that in every room there is a relationship with the outside."

PREVIOUS PAGES AND LEFT: The doors to the bedroom were salvaged from the original home. Sandra added the headboards to a trundle bed set she bought when the family was living in Switzerland. She topped them with her favorite linens. "I love layers of fresh and interesting bedding," she says. "And I am not one to match all the layers, so they are just a mix of soft and cozy ones I have collected along the way."

She is also very partial to that room: "If it's snowing and we are stuck at home I love how the space feels. You can see what's happening as if you were right out there in the elements, yet you are warm and cozy. It's an incredible feeling." The window shades are simple flat linen panels with a swag of burlap to soften the bottom and filter the sunlight. There are roller shades behind them for practicality. The small chandelier is wrapped with chicken wire.

ABOVE LEFT: The wood poles are called "winter sticks" and are used for marking boat moorings during the winter months instead of the small round buoys. "My son found them washed up on the beach and knew I would love them," Sandra says.

ABOVE RIGHT: A fishnet makes a graphic statement. "These are easy to find on Cape Cod," Sandra confides. "They are very versatile and I often layer them over tablecloths, curtains, and even light fixtures." The airy material is also a good match for the wicker chair.

ABOVE: When adding color, Sandra sticks to blue accents only. "Because," she explains, "we have so many windows, the view itself makes the statement."

ABOVE RIGHT: With its wool rug and high-back wicker chairs snuggling up to the fireplace, the library is all about comfort. Shells, corals, and sea fans from Sandra's collection tie the space to its coastal heritage. "It's natural, organic, and easy on the eye," she says. "I want my home to feel quiet and peaceful. And I love that in every room there is a relationship with the outside." The library's furnishings welcome both rustic and modern. Contemporary globe lights from Galotti and Radice cohabit harmoniously with the rustic fireplace reconstructed with the granite bulkhead stones salvaged from the old house and Sandra's prized "Private Beach" sign from a local junk shop. "The owner didn't want to sell it but I worked on him for years until one day he finally agreed," she recalls. In the foyer, a leaded glass transom was added to the recycled doors to allow the beautiful light to stream in throughout the day.

a decorated one," she says. "Collections tell our personal story, the things that pique my interest are those that share the common thread of design excellence—whether it's a seashell, a sofa, or a mirror, lines, colors, and proportions all speak to me."

The Cavallos have travelled far and wide and the places they have visited have had an impact on Sandra's style. "I enjoy experiencing new places and cultures, always taking design influence from the journey. This undoubtedly, is the root of my vintage-modern-mix design style," Sandra notes. "I bought or found many of the pieces at salvage yards and junk shops, including bathroom fixtures, cabinet and door hardware, lighting, and newel posts." Sandra is a true Renaissance woman who loves a variety of styles and eras. "I always find myself looking at primitive New England furniture—but then I can't pass a classic modern piece without my heart skipping a beat! I am also passionate about modern Italian design," she admits. "If you collect things you love, I believe you can make all elements work together in your own personal style statement. Our home is our 'book' and everything in it tells a story."

Sandra and Phil have indeed built more than a home, they have created a legacy for the next generation.

FAR LEFT: Sandra bought the antique runner from Bavaria in a small home decor shop in Zurich, Switzerland where the family lived for a while.

LEFT: The family harvested the stones in the kitchen fireplace from the property, along with the West Falmouth pink granite slab that forms the foundation for the pizza oven. The white oak mantel was left over from the restoration of the SS Constitution. Contemporary chairs with natural linen slipcovers pair up with an oak table from Australia. "The shop had a 50% off Black Friday sale and free shipping worldwide! I couldn't pass it up!" Sandra says. The Dutch doors were chosen because they open up to the view of the tidal estuary

LEFT: The modern kitchen adds a sleek vibe to the cottage's style. The bank of windows overlooks the Herring River salt marsh. A built-in shelf holds a beautiful display of Sandra's shells and corals. "I have been collecting them for years," she says. "I find some in antique and junk shops and some were found on the beach."

ABOVE LEFT: The primitive hutch wears its original milk paint. Sandra found it in Pennsylvania twenty-five years ago. The wood fish is another piece from a local junkyard.

ABOVE RIGHT: When Sandra brought home the vintage buffet she had scored at the world famous Brimfield Flea Market, she called on her friend and artist Michele LaCamera's paint refinishing skills to tweak the color a bit. "Michele has a great eye and knows just what to do," Sandra remarks. The natural undyed wool rug Sandra named "Awning Stripe" is from her very own new online shop. Flea-market oars, primitive paintings, and a classic chandelier bring a nostalgic mood to the charming nook.

LEFT: Glass floats and bottles supply a gentle dose of color reminiscent of the ocean.

RIGHT: In the living room vintage and modern juxtapose to create a space that is at once sophisticated and friendly. Though twenty years old, the sofa, from B&B Italia, looks contemporary. "The great thing about it is that the cover comes off so you can swap out the fabric whenever you want," Sandra says. The rug from Kymo, a German company of contemporary floorwear, provides a quiet foundation for the space and is one of her favorites. A wool pouf adds another layer of texture and comfort. The bronze coffee table was discovered in a junk shop, and Sandra added the wooden top. The sputnik-like chandelier takes on a new dimension with a geometric enclosure. The ladder was rescued from a trip to the dump.

LEFT: The backyard is Carol's favorite space. "Living in Southern California, our garden is the most used 'room' all year round. It's bright, colorful, and I love sitting outside on sunny days listening to the waves," she says. Some of Steve's surfboards testify to his love of the sport. The quaint shed was a gift to Carol from her husband. "One year Steve asked me what I wanted for Christmas and I told him a "house". I sent him a photo of a cute little shed. By that afternoon he had bartered with a dear friend—a painting for the building of the shed!" Carol recalls. "The door was a donation from a friend." The blue trim, red door, and flags nod to Carole's affection for primary colors.

flip flop escape

VENTURA, CA

You could say that for Carol and Steve Cook, the love of the coast is in their DNA. The California duo has traveled from Jamaica to Hawaii, Costa Rica, Mexico, and other areas where Steve, a passionate surfer, could indulge his love of the sport.

When their children were born, the couple settled on the West Coast to raise their family and pursue careers in education and art. With retirement came the need to downsize. By then the Cooks already had one child in college and the other headed there soon. They opted to move into a small beach cottage in Ventura, California. "We wanted to live at the beach. Our daughter was

a competitive surfer and she wanted to be able to check the surf and get in a few waves before school. Our goal was to stay in the area and Pierpont Beach is the only beach community in Ventura," Carol explains.

The quaintness and location of the 1928 cottage reminded Carol of the homes of her youth. "I grew up going to Laguna Beach to visit relatives and I loved the cottage they lived in. We wanted a similar one with interesting features. The mullioned windows were the first things I noticed," she recalls. However moving from a spacious home to a 950 square-foot cottage came with some challenges. "We just used the furniture from our much larger home. It was a tight fit and some of my favorite family pieces went to my sister," Carol notes.

Over time larger pieces have been replaced with items more proportional to the small space. The mix of furnishings and coastal elements give the home its unique flavor. The decor mirrors Carol's vision. "We want our home to say: 'We are glad you are here. Don't worry about tracking in some sand!'"

ABOVE: The back fence doubles as a whimsical art gallery displaying found items like the California license plate and the buoys picked up on the beach. PAPA SRF is a personalized plate belonging to Steve who made the BEACH sign from a piece of driftwood and fashioned the peace sign with sea glass.

RIGHT: The yellow kneeboard was a down payment for a painting commissioned by a friend of Steve. Shells and nautical weights pay tribute to the cottage location. True to her love of red, white, and blue, and vintage, Carol hung little buoys on a salvaged window.

RIGHT: "Steve's paintings are sought by collectors, and Firestone Vineyard in Santa Barbara even showcased his work on their wine labels. Our home also serves as his art gallery," Carol explains. "The art is ever changing as paintings sell. He also creates work for me—both the buoys painting ('Carol's Buoys') and the surfboard painting ('Rasta Bonzer') were specifically executed to fit in the tall narrow spaces they occupy on either side of the living room windows."

Carol keeps the decor simple but cozy. Vintage pieces like the former red hospital cart and a well-loved flea market leather armchair convey a nostalgic charm. Red, white, and blue accents bring in cheerful notes.

White walls provide a soothing backdrop for splashes of color. "I used to favor bold colors, but now I am focusing on blue and white and only bring in primary color in accent pieces," says Carol, who credits her beach-inspired decorating to the coastal location. "We found the shells and the buoys on our morning beach walks." Carol likes to take her time finding the right pieces and accessories. "I am curating our belongings down to just what we love and need."

Steve's paintings also play a major role in the Cooks' home. "Steve has been sketching since he was a little boy—his mother was an artist and there were always supplies to promote creativity," Carole explains. "He says that this house really brought out his muse. He started painting on surfboards and took them to a gallery—they all sold quickly. In 2002 he began taking classes at the local college where his professors

ABOVE LEFT: Of the pair of shells dressing the mantel, the right one holds a very special place in Carol's heart. "It is from my husband's Maldives surf trip in 2001," she recalls. "When he booked the trip eight months before, we didn't realize that our 30th anniversary would fall during the three weeks he would be gone. This was not a vacation where he would be visiting any shops to bring me home a souvenir. A fisherman noticed Steve's binoculars and asked him how much he would take for them. Steve said all he wanted was a pretty shell to take home to me. It was the perfect trade and the perfect gift!"

ABOVE RIGHT: A reproduction of an old metal shopping cart holds starfish and shells collected on the beach.

RIGHT: Above the slipcovered loveseat a painting holds vacation memories and pride of place. "During a family reunion in Northern California, we rode our bikes past the colorful houseboats in Sausalito. I asked Steve to stop and snap a few photos. From those he painted this piece 'Just a Houseboat in Sausalito,'" Carol says. The makeshift coffee table was made with an orange crate from Carol's family groves. "I found it in my parents' garage," she says. "I decided to strip it and discovered the V.H.O. lettering, which stands for Valencia Heights Orchards. Steve made the top for it and I use the inside for storage."

recognized his natural talents. Eventually he quit his day job to simply paint. He used to display his work in multiple shows at a time, but when I retired he cut back to give us time to play. He still shows a bit and takes on commissions, but mostly he just paints what he wants." As for Carol, she wants her home to be filled with pieces with a history but also to reflect hers and Steve's personalities and interests. "I really believe a house should tell a story, and as such it's always a work in progress!" she happily says.

ABOVE: With space as a premium Steve designed the plate rack. "It provides storage and also makes the room look larger," Carol says.

ABOVE RIGHT: Shells, sand, and sea glass picked up on the beach become decorative accents spilling from green glass vessels.

RIGHT: Steve built the tabletop from 100-year-old barn wood found at a ranch that sold salvaged wood. The chairs have seen several colors but now sport deep blue and white finishes. The shelf holds an ever-changing display of favorite seasonal items. The window seat was added to offer more seating space in the narrow dining room and also storage. "It's not only where we eat but it's also where I read or work on my blog and photography," Carol explains. "The name of the painting is 'Hanalei Nobility'. It's an old plantation house sitting right on Hanalei Bay in Hawaii. It is Steve's favorite of all his paintings. We have spent many family vacations right there on Hanalei Bay and the painting holds precious memories."

"We want our home to say: 'We are glad you are here. Don't worry about tracking in some sand!'"

PREVIOUS PAGES: When the Cooks replaced the living room windows they saved one to use as the headboard in the bedroom. When Carol's daughter-in-law first saw 'Summertime', Steve's rendition of a beach called Marina Park, she recognized the setting and exclaimed, "That's my childhood!" Carol found the hutch in its present condition. "Maybe one day I will paint it, but I love the soft pastel," she muses. A quilt from a local shop echoes the blue and white hues of cresting waves.

ABOVE: Soft aqua glass bottles and little beach shovels add endearing touches. "The shovels came with reproduction beach buckets that are holding plants around the house. I just love the vintage designs." Carol notes.

RIGHT: Originally two shades of gray, Carol painted the blue dresser to fit the room color scheme. Another example of Steve's work is based on a photo of a family Christmas in Kauai, Hawaii. "The people on the beach are our son, daughter, and me," Carol explains. "The title is 'The Descendants of the Artist at Hanalei.' It was named after the movie, The Descendants, which was filmed in Hanalei."

FAR RIGHT: Carol cherishes the pillow that she made from a handkerchief, a gift from one of her many blogging friends. Rather than tuck it away she sewed it onto a white linen pillow.

LEFT: With its fireplace, pine beams, and cheerful colors, the cozy sitting room is where Michele and David like to hang out during the winter months. Michele has a soft spot for the mid-century chairs. "I love them because they are comfortable and petite," she says. "Nantucket Red is a popular color on Cape Cod and nearby islands. I found the fun fabric, which then solidified my decision to paint the chairs that specific hue." The original brick wall was painted bright white to lighten the room. For extra texture and comfort, a circa-1950 handmade Turkish rug is layered over a neutral sisal. Michele found the 150-year-old coffee table in an antique shop and kept it in its original condition.

seaside comforts

CAPE COD, MA

Michele LaCamera and David Buckley share a mutual affection for Cape Cod where Michele loves to swim and David surf. Luckily, when the time came to buy a cottage they found just the right one in historic West Falmouth.

"It wasn't our first home but it was our first together," Michele says. "I owned a smaller house on the Cape and David downsized from a larger one in Virginia Beach." After looking in several towns, they both agreed they loved the area with its harbor, beaches, salt air, and "old Cape Cod" feel. "We sold our homes and bought the cottage together," Michele says. "It was in a lovely neighborhood with quaint shops, and though it was dated it had obvious potential." With David's skills and her background in art she knew they could make it work.

Michele's passion for creativity in several mediums of art led her to the New England School of Art and Design where she studied interior design, use of color, and lighting, as well as various painting techniques. It didn't take long for friends and acquaintances to seek her skills and talents, and soon after she started her own custom painting furniture business. "I gravitate to vintage and antique furniture," she says. "I am drawn toward giving new life to old or unwanted pieces that are just crying to be made beautiful again." In fact, the absence of store-bought furniture is apparent in the cottage. "All the pieces are our own creations, hand-painted and reupholstered," she says with pride. "David was instrumental not only in reinventing them but also making them structurally sound when needed." The end result is a comfy beach cottage that is authentic and eclectic.

LEFT: The old beadboard cabinet was scored at a popular local vintage market. Its original chippy gray paint and size appealed to Michele, who later found the pair of oars with a similar finish. "David and I made the flag from the wood of an old park bench," she explains. "He put the structure together and I hand painted it, and then added the final touch with fifty mini starfish to represent the states. It's one of our favorite pieces." The cabinet houses some of Michele's shell and bottle collections and also lends itself to the addition of seasonal items.

RIGHT: The dining room walls are newly redone in shiplap. "The room felt very plain before we added it. Now the space is so much cozier," Michele says. "We found the chandelier in Maine and just liked its unique style. It is a little bit rustic yet perfect for a cottage." Michele collects glass fishing floats for their colors and coastal feel and often uses them to create centerpieces with shells she and her family found on various beaches. "They are reminders of our vacations and special times." Watercolor, oil, acrylic, or charcoal, the seascapes tie with Michele's signature blues and greens. "I love vintage paintings because many were done by amateur painters," she says.

Michele and David like to take their time gathering and reinventing items they love. "It's a practice that has proven more successful than when we hurry through a project," Michele notes. "Whenever we rush, the piece ends up having to be redone." Because she buys and sells furniture as part of her business, Michele has the ability to substitute one piece for another in her home. "Each has story," she says. "David and I love to go antiquing all over New England."

In decorating the home, Michele says that the biggest challenge was blending furniture from different periods together. "If you stick to a color palette you can blend old and new beautifully," she notes. "We have everything from primitive to mid-century modern to newer handmade farm tables. If you walk into a room and it feels cohesive without one piece standing out too much, then you have done a good job blending old and new!" The colors of the ocean, the beach, and the sunsets dictated the color palette, and the coastal location inspired the selection of accessories, hence the shells, driftwood, artwork from local artists, and vintage finds. Nothing appears out of place. All these elements came together in creating a seaside sanctuary filled with authenticity, originality and charm.

The colors of the ocean, the beach, and the sunsets dictated the color palette.

PREVIOUS PAGES AND RIGHT: Michele favors furniture with a past. "I love its history and I enjoy saving it from landfills and making it look pretty," she says. "I always add a few modern touches here or there so it doesn't feel dated." She reupholstered the couch and wing chair in a durable tweed fabric. The antique sea captain's trunk, discovered in an old fishing village shop, was in need of some attention so she painted it with Miss Mustard Seed's Farmhouse White, "I love milk paint for old pieces because it creates a bit of chipping here and there that gives an authentic look," she explains. The armoire was made out of parts from an Amish kitchen. The "Beach House" sign is another product of the couple's joint efforts. "Once again, David created the structure from old wood that we found, and I hand painted it and added starfish. We enjoy doing these types of projects together on weekends," Michele says.

LEFT: Glass orbs and a wispy coastal plant were chosen for their maritime relevance.

BELOW: The buffet is made from two cabinets placed side by side. "We added the feet and refinished a nice piece of pine wood for the top," Michele says. "It works well against the shiplap which was added as an accent wall. We have b[een] incorporating more architectural interest to eac[h] space as the years go on." The lanterns hangin[g] from heavy-duty brackets recall the old ones fishermen used. David has ben surfing since he [was] a kid and the Shark Bay Balsa surfboard from Ecuador awaits the summer waves.

ABOVE: "For this bedroom we wanted a more tropical, beach vibe, one where our guests felt like they were truly away," Michele explains. " I went with aqua accents to represent the ocean and bring out the blue from the quilt."

RIGHT: The cabinet was one of the first pieces Michele painted in Provence by Annie Sloan Chalk Paint, a favorite color she used on several pieces throughout the house. The oar, a housewarming gift from a friend, turned out to be a perfect companion for the cabinet.

FAR RIGHT: Michele chose to enhance the room's natural light with bright white and gentle color accents to set a soothing tone. The formerly black iron bed got a new fresh look with Annie Sloan Chalk Paint. Shells, glass bottles, and a wooden whale communicate the seaside location. On the bedside table a hand-blown vase from Martha's Vineyard Glasswork has great sentimental value for Michele. It holds a delicate coral fan that contrasts beautifully with its lustrous blue and green hues. The table's base features a pineapple, which is symbolic of hospitality.

family style

SANTA BARBARA, CA

When the owners of a guest cottage wanted to update their home into a perfect vacation escape, they turned to designer Jodi Goldberg who knew exactly how to create a fun and comfortable living space that would highlight its ocean location.

"Merely steps from the couple's main house and close to the neighboring children's homes, they thought it would be an ideal gathering space for the family," says Jodi, who suggested a beach house concept to showcase the ocean and Santa Barbara. "I wanted the space to feel completely different from the main house, a place where they could kick off their shoes and relax."

The original cottage was gutted to create a more open space with sweeping coastal views. "It's quintessential West Coast," says Jodi whose clever approach to space, attention to detail, and an affinity for tactile finishes epitomize Santa Barbara chic.

Awash in white and blue the beach house's vibrant rooms flow together with a color palette in hues sympathetic to its seaside location while focusing on providing the comfort and warmth of a vacation escape shared with family. "Consistency between rooms is important," Jodi notes. "I used a variety of textures and tones, but maintained a blue palette throughout the house. While everything shouldn't be the same color, the palettes used from room to room should flow harmoniously. Color from a painting, rug, or lamp can add visual interest to a space and tie in other colors from the room."

Jodi's fine-tuned sensitivity towards her clients' needs shines in the way she made use of their art collection and added custom-designed furnishings to give the house the feel of a family-friendly vacation getaway.

She collaborated with the couple to hand-select fabrics, artwork, and one-of-a-kind pieces to invigorate the space and give the home layers of interest, color, and texture. A unifying palette exists within the space, creating a seamless environment that feels light and welcoming. Another design goal was for the inside to flow seamlessly with the outdoors.

ABOVE: A whimsical and colorful mosaic mermaid honors the oceanic location. It's indicative of the homeowners' love of art, which they embrace in its many forms outside as well as inside.

RIGHT: A custom-made sign announces the entrance to the property while a mosaic by artist Tami Macala represents the owners' families: the lion symbolizes the grandfather, the sun represents the grandmother, and the whales' tails stand for their two families. The three stars at the bottom are for the three grandchildren, the American flag for their son and the other for their Danish daughter-in-law.

LEFT: An abstract painting by Santa Barbara artist Karen Bezuidenhout exudes the peaceful beauty of the coast through stylized sailboats. Found lobster warps are fashioned into tassels on the driftwood bench created by Michael Fleming. A tall wood bottle complements the organic feel of the entry.

RIGHT: In the hallway to the bedroom a mosaic surfboard by artist Tami Macala shows appreciation for the sport and sea life.

BELOW: The foyer welcomes with a framed surfboard photo depicting iconic boards and eras, a gift to the homeowners from the Surfboard Museum. A pair of lamps with rope-wrapped bases flanks a trio of graceful aquatic sculptures in similar colors and finishes.

"I love connecting the in and the out," she says. "The views are magnificent, and there are tons of entertainment spaces...so many places to be happy in that house!"

Jodi gave her clients exactly what they wanted: a coastal getaway and a welcome refuge for friends and family, Driftwood Beach House inspires hospitality from its insightful design and the vivacious spirit of its family.

"While everything shouldn't be the same color, the palettes used from room to room should flow harmoniously."

RIGHT: A chandelier by the South African artist Riaan Chambers presides over contemporary chairs and an acacia dining room table from Bali. This one-of-a-kind chandelier was created with clear, white, aqua, green, and blue sea glass suspended by thin wiring. The homeowners selected the patchwork of the vintage Turkish rug for their range of blues. Naturally bleached driftwood is made into a simple but sculptural candleholder.

FAR RIGHT: The ample coffee table combines the rustic beauty of natural petrified wood inlaid in a mosaic pattern with the modernity of the stainless steel base.

LEFT: "My clients trusted me to create a specific style, feel, and vibe, but we worked hand-in-hand to select each piece," Jodi says. The white backdrop of the sleek and spacious living room allows the coast-inspired blue hues and the art to take center stage. "The homeowners love art and are serious collectors. This design showcases their existing collection and seamlessly integrates new commissioned pieces. I was very intentional with this design aspect," Jodi notes. The decor reflects the sea with accessories, and organic elements fashioned into interesting pieces, like stools that recall lobster traps.

ABOVE: Integrating the design with items indigenous to the coast is present in every room. Here a grouping of shells of similar size and color make a simple but authentic statement.

RIGHT: An artwork by Michael Fleming featuring salvaged lobster warps in white and blues is the den's focal point. The batik pillows bring added visual impact and comfort to the sectional. The petrified wood coffee table holds an assortment of sea-related accents.

TOP FAR RIGHT: From the chair upholstered in ikat to the pillows, throw, and rug, blue, turquoise, and aqua hues bring the ocean to the bedroom. The hammered silver stool adds shimmer and the stone-topped bedside table injects a modern touch. An oil on canvass by the artist Sherri Belassen, who uses shapes and colors in a contemporary manner to create her unique artwork like these surfers' silhouettes, is a perfectly fitting piece for a home that is all about art, surfing, and fun.

BOTTOM FAR RIGHT: The pillows' combination of small and large patterns, varied fabrics, textures, sizes, and a mix of bold and soft colors work well together because they pull from the art in the room.

classic charm

ST. GEORGE, ME

After years of living in the Washington, DC area Molly and John Walpuck decided to move their family to the rugged coast of Maine.

Growing up, Molly had spent many summers on Nantucket, and also went to college in New England. "I fell in love with the state and have always wanted to return there," she says. The property they bought in Tenants Harbor on the St. George peninsula came with two small cottages that had been moved from another location earlier on. "They were both run down," Molly says. "We kept and renovated the small one and demolished the other. We then designed and built the main house. We tried to use local materials, or at least typical to Maine. Natural cedar shingles are a classic finish for New England coastal homes," she explains. "I love how they will change color and gain patina as they age."

LEFT: The original small cottage was remodeled and now welcomes Molly's many friends who are eager to visit in the summer. "It's totally independent from the main house but has all the necessary amenities and it is very private," Molly says. The exterior's new cedar shingles have already begun to weather while those protected by the overhang will take longer to get the same patina. Buoys are painted with numbers that identify the house's street address. Maddie, one of the family's two English Springer Spaniels, strikes a pose on the porch.

ABOVE: Depending on weather conditions (and one's mood), surfboards, paddle boards, and kayaks standby for a day of fun.

"If you live on the coast of Maine you have to have a buoy collection."

FAR LEFT: Colorful weathered buoys give the garden shed a festive flair. "Not all the buoys I use are old." Molly says. "I have gotten them from various places—flea markets, antique shows, and some have just washed up on the shoreline."

LEFT: "If you live on the coast of Maine you have to have a buoy collection," Molly explains. "The villages of Tenants Harbor, Port Clyde, and Martinsville have large lobstering industries. In the summer there are thousands of lobster buoys dotting the water!"

The location also drove Molly's decorating scheme. "I wanted the view to take center stage and the interior to complement it," she says. She chose the blues, tans, and grays of the water, rocks, and sky to keep pace with the inspiring vistas, and accessorized with items that recall the home's natural surroundings. "I have always had a love of nautical decor, so my collections include shells, fish, and seagulls," she notes. The mix of classic details and a marine palette channels the coastal landscape and allows the home's rustic beauty and traditional character to shine.

"Decorating this home actually came really easily to me," Molly notes. "I think that when a space reflects nature it develops organically. There is nothing artificial or contrived here—the colors and materials are all natural."

When entering Molly's home her love affair with blue is evident. "You can say I have a thing for it and its many variations!" she readily admits. "Since most of the downstairs is one open space, I wanted the colors to flow throughout so I used different shades of the same blue tone in all the elements—walls, paneling, textiles, even the kitchen backsplash tiles."

As for furniture, Molly prefers to support local businesses. "It is particularly important in small communities," she says. "I got the majority right here in Maine, all the soft furnishings are from a local furniture store in Warren, the lighting came from Portland, and the dining room table was made by New England Joinery in Monmouth." The vintage and antique pieces and accessories are from local auction houses and antique stores as well.

Molly is also big on comfort and function. "Everything in my home is meant to be used and is designed for comfort. Nothing is too precious. Dogs are allowed on the furniture. Pillows can be tossed on the floor when not in use. I prefer vintage and antique pieces with some wear to them so that I don't have to fret about something getting banged up or scratched."

ABOVE LEFT: Molly loves to cook and the kitchen was designed to accommodate her needs and family meals. With a quartz top and plenty of storage within the natural red birch cabinets, the spacious island provides ample space for prep and casual meals. The pot rack, made from brass plumbing parts, keeps pans out of the way but readily available. Molly painted the pantry doors a dramatic deep blue to make it appear like a free-standing piece of furniture. The woven plastic seats of the rattan stools (from Serena and Lily) add to the kitchen's blue and white color theme.

ABOVE RIGHT: "I just started collecting these fish molds recently," Molly says. "I got a couple from local antique stores and thought it would be fun to do a whole wall with them. I have built my collection from Etsy, Ebay, and different antique shows. I love the interplay of shapes and materials. And of course they are another nod to our coastal location."

RIGHT: With a bank of windows overlooking a deck and the waters of Mosquito Harbor the dining room seems like a decorated extension of the outdoors. Faithful to her palette, Molly imbued the room with cool blues and warm tans, and her trademark mix of textures and patterns. The reclaimed pine table was custom-made to be the setting for meals with family and friends for years to come. The chandelier was chosen for its classic lines and size. "I particularly like how it doesn't obscure the view," Molly says.

ABOVE LEFT: The double-sided fireplace between the kitchen and a sitting room was built with granite stones discovered and salvaged when the foundation for the house was dug. The mantel, recycled from the old cottage, was embellished with small shells and rocks from local beaches. The work of an amateur artist, the painting depicts the Portland Head Light that was built in the early 1790s. The seascape brings home the scenic beauty and colors of the coast.

ABOVE RIGHT: "I did not personally collect the shells from the seashore, but I did acquire all of them from various places over a long period of times," says Molly, who also bought the etchings at an auction. The shell-decorated anchor is akin to a sailors' Valentine, which were often souvenirs from seaside locations during the Victorian era. The chest of drawers is one of Molly's favorite pieces and quite the bargain. "It probably dates to the late 1800s. I got it at a local auction for just $30. I was ready to fight for it, but I was the only bidder!" she recounts. "I love the original faux wood grain painted finish and the sweet pastoral scenes in the middle of each drawer."

"Everything in my home is meant to be used and is designed for comfort."

ABOVE: A soft blue and white color scheme gives the living room a tranquil vibe. "I love the play of pattern and color. It makes a space much more interesting," she says. "It is fun to come up with a combination that works. My true love is fabric—I can never pick just one, so I combine multiple." Deciding what would go on the wall over the couch proved to be a bit of a challenge. "I had seen and admired gallery walls of modern prints of the Swedish artist Olof Rudbeck's bird etchings," Molly says. "I toyed with various combinations of smaller prints for quite a while, but ultimately decided to go big for impact compared to the other gallery groupings in the room. I went with a seagull for obvious reasons. I absolutely adore it!"

Her decor combines two of her favorite styles: the structure and geometry of classic pieces and the informality of cottage style. Molly defines her look as New England traditional meets relaxed cottage. It is a true reflection of who she is. "I love that when someone walks into my home they immediately gain a sense of both person and place. I worked as an analyst for the government for my entire career—my home was always my creative outlet," she explains. She also gravitates to the ocean. "The water brings me peace. It both grounds me and lifts me up," she says. "I love to watch the ebb and flow of the tides, the different moods of the coastline, and the birds in action. I also enjoy watching human interaction with the water—the lobster boats hauling traps, and sailboats, kayakers, and paddle boarders gliding by. I love the informality and spontaneity of life here."

LEFT: Molly wanted a feature wall to delineate the sleeping nook from the rest of the one-room guesthouse. "It also needed to be an accent color to make it pop, so I drew on some of the red accessories in the cottage," she says. The bedding illustrates her love for mixing patterns. "I thought the pillows with their whale design were a fun idea for a coastal cottage!" The shadow box is a replica of a large sailing ship that was built in Rockland, the nearest "large" town. A black antique minnow bucket, a gift from a friend, adds a graphic note to a vintage wicker side table Molly refreshed with a coat of red. The bench at the foot of the bed is also an antique.

RIGHT: Molly painted the pine floor of the bathroom with a custom color oil paint. "I had to do it twice because the first blue wasn't quite right!" she says. The antique wicker chair is a perfect companion to the graceful lines of the curvaceous shelf. The shower curtain was custom made but the towels are from Target and HomeGoods.

FAR RIGHT: For the bathroom Molly wanted a modern version of a classic Maine bathroom cottage. To that end she opted for paneled walls, painted wood floor, and a marble vanity with retro nickel supports. Blue and white baskets hold toiletries with style.

index

Page numbers in *italics* refer to illustrations

A

Acheson, Jenny 64–71
Albini, Franco 32
Anna Maria Island, Florida 34–43
art collections 71, *82, 85, 114, 116–17*, 129, *138, 138, 144–5*

B

Beck, Jody 34–43
Belassen, Sherri *147*
Benjamin Moore 29, *49, 51*
Bezuidenhout, Karen *140*
blues *11, 12, 16, 16, 21, 32, 63, 106, 134*, 138, *144–5*, 151
Buckley, David 126–35
buoys 17, *17, 115*, 118, *148, 150–1*
Burns, Elizabeth 82–95
Burns, Kelsey 93
Burns, Kevin 93

C

Cape Cod, Massachusetts 44–53, 96–111, 126–35
Carlson, Nikki and Steve 72–81
Cassill, Tania 24–33
Cavallo, Gianni 99, 105
Cavallo, Nathalie 99
Cavallo, Phil 97, 107
Cavallo, Sandra 96–111
Chambers, Riaan *142*

chandeliers *33, 45, 60, 63, 104, 110, 111, 129, 142, 153*
Clark, Alex 75
colors 10–12, *20, 34, 35, 38–9*, 118, 156
Constitution, SS 107
Cook, Carol and Steve 112–25
coral 15, *21, 91, 106, 108–9*
Cottage + Sea 72–81
Crawford, Ilse 24

D

decks *26–7, 38–9*
driftwood 19, *19, 31, 51*, 93, *114*, 129, *142*
Driftwood Beach House 136–47

E

edb Designs 90
embellishments 13–19
Encinitas, California 72–81

F

Farrow & Ball 29
fire pits *78–9*, 95
fireplaces 59, *106, 107, 154*
Firestone Vineyard 116
fish moulds 152
fishing floats 18, *18, 99, 110, 129*
fishnets *105*
Fleming, Michael *140, 146–7*
furnishings 20–1

G

glass
  fishing floats 18, *18, 99, 110, 129*
  sea glass 16, *16, 30, 62, 85, 87, 90, 93*, 93, *114, 120*
Goldberg, Jodi 54–63, 137–47

H

Hanna, Jimmy and Julia 24–33
Heller, Mark and Rosa 34–43
Hicks, Lisa and Ken 44–53

K

Kauai, Hawaii 124–5

L

LaCamera, Michele 110, 126–35
Laguna Beach, California 24–33, 114
Lido Beach, Florida 64–71
lighting, chandeliers *33, 45, 60, 63, 104, 110, 111, 129, 142, 153*
The Little Glass House 82–95

M

Macala, Tami *139, 141*
Macchi, Rob and Gayle 45–7
McCobb, Paul 68
Malin, Gray 31, *32*
Meadow Rose Photography *63*
mid-century modern 68, 71, 76, 90, 93, *126*, 129

N

neutrals *12, 21, 58, 62, 72–3*, 93
New England Joinery 152
New England School of Art and Design 127

P

Portland Head Light *154*

R

Rieke, Dale 64–71
Rudbeck, Olof *155*

S

St. George, Maine 148–57
Santa Barbara, California 54–63, 82–95, 136–47
sea glass 16, *16, 30, 62, 85, 87, 90, 93*, 93, *114, 120*
seating 20, *20, 21, 38–9*, 44, 45, *68–9, 130–1*
  outdoor *56–7, 66–7*
shells 15, *15, 21, 37, 91*, 93, *106, 108–9*, 115, 118, *118, 120*, 129, *135, 146, 154*
Sherwin Williams *42*
showers, outdoor *94, 100–1*
Sloan, Annie *134, 135*
soft furnishings 20–1
starfish 15, 16, *16, 91*, 118, *130–1*
storage *38–9, 84–5, 120, 121*
sunset hues 10
Surfboard Museum *140*
surfboards 13–14, *66, 71*, 76, *78–9, 89, 94, 113, 132, 136, 140, 149*

T

texture *20, 58, 62*
turquoise 11, 16, *16*

V

Ventura, California 112–25

W

Walpuck, John & Molly 148–57
Weilbacher, Tara 93
whites *10, 77*, 118

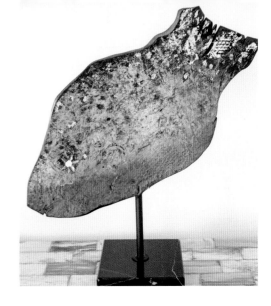

resources

CHAPTER 1 SHACK CHIC

huit Laguna
www.huitlaguna.com

CHAPTER 2 ISLAND VERNACULAR

The Surof House
www.amilocals.com/anna-maria-island-rentals/
The-Surof-House

Traction Architecture
www.tractionarchitecture.com

CHAPTER 3 TINY HAVEN

Lisa Hicks Interiors
www.lisahicksinteriors.com

CHAPTER 4 SEASIDE ZEN

Jodi G Designs
www.jodigdesigns.com

CHAPTER 5 COASTAL VIBES

Wood Street Studios
www.woodstreetstudios.com

Jenny Acheson Photography
www.jennyacheson.com

Lido Beach House
www.lidobeachhouse.com/

Shine Shine
www.shineshine.co.za

CHAPTER 6 FREE SPIRIT

COTTAGE + SEA
www.cottageandsea.com
www.instagram.com/cottageandsea

CB2
www.cb2.com

World Market
www.worldmarket.com

Kaekoo
www.kaekoo.com

The Loomia
www.theloomia.com

Kip&Co
www.kipandco.com

Olive & Linen
www.oliveandlinen.com

Pottery Barn
www.potterybarn.com

Bliss 101
store.bliss101.com

Timberwave
www.timberwave.ca

Petite Lily Interiors
www.petitelilyinteriors.fr/en

Wayfair
www.wayfair.com

CHAPTER 7 SERENE SENSIBILITY

edb designs
www.edbdesignssb.com
www.instagram.com/edbdesigns

Mate Gallery
www.mategallery.com

Sonoma Cottage Home
www.instagram.com/sonomacottagehome

Porch
www.porchsb.com

Patine
www.patinedecor.com

CHAPTER 8 SEAWORTHY SANCTUARY

Vintage Reclaimed
www.vintagefurniturereclaimed.com
www.instagram.com/vintagefurniturereclaimed

Old Silver Shed
www.oldsilvershed.com/online-store
www.instagram.com/oldsilvershed

CHAPTER 9 FLIP FLOP ESCAPE

Steve Cook Studio
www.stevecookstudio.com

Art and Sand
www.artandsand.blogspot.com

CHAPTER 10 SEASIDE COMFORTS

Vintage Reclaimed
www.vintagefurniturereclaimed.com

CHAPTER 11 FAMILY STYLE

Jodi G Designs
www.jodigdesigns.com

Designs Adrift
www.designsadrift.com

Karen Bezuidenhout
www.facebook.com/Karen-Bezuidenhout-
Art-148989015157934/

All Cracked Up Mosaic
www.allcrackedupmosaics.com

Sherri Belassen
www.sherribelassen.com

CHAPTER 12 CLASSIC CHARM

Molly in Maine
www.instagram.com/mollyinmaine

ADDITIONAL RESOURCES

Roberts Surfboards
www.robertssurf.com

Hansen Surfboards
www.hansensurf.com

ACKNOWLEDGMENTS

Creating a book is a labor of love. What begins with an idea and a theme can only come to fruition through an intimate collaboration with many highly skilled people. My heartfelt thanks to Cindy Richards for trusting me once again, Sally Powell for your artistry, Martha Gavin for being so gentle with editing, Gillian Haslam for her expert proofreading, and Gordana Simakovic for skillfully managing the production of the book.

My sincere thanks also go to all the inspiring homeowners, designers, and makers who welcomed us into their lives: Jenny Acheson and Dale Rieke, Elizabeth Burns, Nikki and Steve Carlson, Tania Cassill, Sandra and Phil Cavallo, Carol and Steve Cook, Jodi Goldberg, Julia and Jimmy Hanna, Mark and Rosa Heller, Lisa Hicks and Ken Kolodziej, Michele LaCamera and David Buckley, Molly and John Walpuck, and Robert Weiner. Photographing your homes, and getting to know you and your stories, was delightful and rewarding.

Last but definitively not least, working with photographer Mark Lohman was the icing on the cake. Mark, you always go above and beyond and your work perfectly illustrates the saying "a picture is worth a thousand words." Thank you.

With much love and appreciation.

Fifi